BOOK WORMS

Earth Matters
Air

Dana Meachen Rau

mc Marshall Cavendish
Benchmark
New York

We cannot see air. But air is all around us. We breathe air. We need air to live on Earth.

Air covers the whole Earth.
This air is called the *atmosphere*.

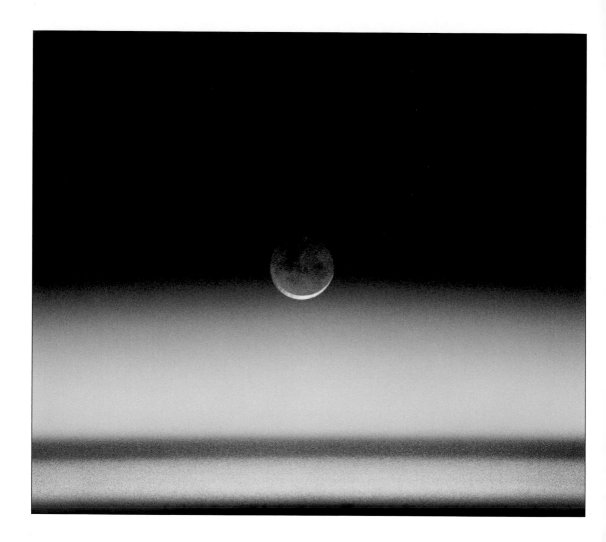

6

The atmosphere stretches more than 300 miles (500 km) above Earth. Driving that far in a car would take more than five hours!

The atmosphere is made of many kinds of *gases*. We cannot see these gases. But we breathe them. There would be no life on Earth without the gases of the atmosphere.

The atmosphere gives us a gas called *oxygen*. We need oxygen for our bodies to work. Outer space does not have oxygen. That is why *astronauts* wear special suits in space.

The atmosphere helps keep Earth warm. Heat from the Sun warms Earth. The atmosphere keeps that heat from going back into space. People, animals, and plants need this heat to live.

The Sun gives off harmful *rays*, too. The atmosphere keeps us safe from some of these rays.

The part of the atmosphere closest to Earth is very active. Many types of weather happen here. Air can be warm or cold. A *thermometer* tells us how warm or cold air is.

18

Air also has *weight*. Air pushes down on Earth. This is called *air pressure*.

Air pressure can make wind.
Cool air is heavy and moves
down. Warm air is light and
moves up.

As this air moves, it makes wind.

Wind can move fast or slow. Wind can come from any direction. A *weather vane* shows where the wind is blowing from.

23

You find clouds in the atmosphere. Clouds are made of water. They can be flat or puffy.

You can fly above the clouds in an airplane.

Drops of water from clouds can fall to the ground. If the air is warm, they fall as rain.

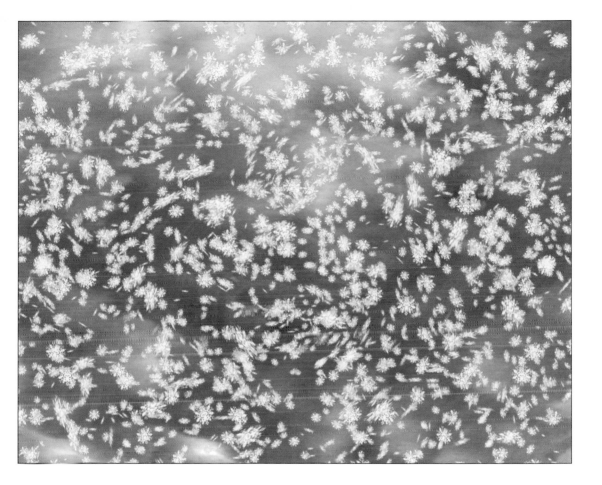

If the air is cold, they fall as snow.

Take a breath. Fly a kite. Enjoy the air around you.

Challenge Words

air pressure (air PRESH-ehr)—Air pushing down on Earth.

astronauts (AS-truh-nots)—People who travel in and explore space.

atmosphere (AT-muhs-fir)—The layer of gases surrounding Earth.

gas—A form of matter we cannot see.

oxygen (OKS-i-jehn)—A gas we need to breathe to live.

rays (rayz)—Lines of light.

thermometer (thehr-MOM-eh-tehr)—A tool that tells us how warm or cold air is.

weather vane (WETH-uhr vane)—A tool that tells us the direction of the wind.

weight (wayt)—How heavy or light something is.

Index

Page numbers in **boldface** are illustrations.

With thanks to Nanci Vargus, Ed.D., and Beth Walker Gambro, reading consultants

Marshall Cavendish Benchmark
99 White Plains Road
Tarrytown, New York 10591-5502
www.marshallcavendish.us

Library of Congress Cataloging-in-Publication Data

Rau, Dana Meachen, 1971–
Air / by Dana Meachen Rau.
p. cm. — (Bookworms. Earth matters)
Summary: "Discusses the role of the gases surrounding Earth and the relationship of the atmosphere to weather"—Provided by publisher.
Includes index.
ISBN 978-0-7614-3042-1
1. Atmosphere—Juvenile literature. 2. Weather—Juvenile literature. I. Title.
QC863.5.R379 2008
551.5—dc22
2007030280

Editor: Christina Gardeski
Publisher: Michelle Bisson
Designer: Virginia Pope
Art Director: Anahid Hamparian

Photo Research by Anne Burns Images

Cover Photo by *Corbis*/Guenter Rossenback

The photographs in this book are used with permission and through the courtesy of:
Photo Researchers: p. 1 Carl Purcell; p. 17 Jeff Lepore; p. 20 Carl Purcell. *Alamy Images*: p. 2 RaLuck; p. 21 Giles Angel. *Corbis*: p. 5 G.Boden/zefa; pp. 6, 10 Corbis; p. 9 Tim Davis; pp. 13, 27 Matthias Kulka/zefa; p. 14 Mark Owen Illustration Works; p. 24 Kristy Anne Glubish/Design Pics; p. 25 George Hall; p. 26 Craig Tuttle; p. 29 Ariel Skelley. *Photri/Microstock*: p. 18. *SuperStock*: p. 23 age fotostock.

Printed in Malaysia
1 3 5 6 4 2

JAN   2010